HEALTH HELPERS

VET

URSULA PANG

PowerKiDS press

Published in 2026 by The Rosen Publishing Group, Inc.
2544 Clinton Street, Buffalo, NY 14224

First Edition

Editor: Greg Roza
Book Design: Rachel Rising

Photo Credits: Cover, p.1 SeventyFour/Shutterstock.com; pp. 4, 6, 8, 10, 12, 14, 16, 18, 20 TechSolution/Shutterstock.com; p. 5 Pressmaster/Shutterstock.com; p. 7 Juice Flair/Shutterstock.com; p. 9 Standret/Shutterstock.com; p. 11 Orawan Pattarawimonchai/Shutterstock.com; p. 13 Ekatsyerina Kostsina/Shutterstock.com; p. 13 AlexandruPh/Shutterstock.com; p. 15 Iryna Kalamurza/Shutterstock.com; p. 17 hedgehog94/Shutterstock.com; p. 19 ORION PRODUCTION/Shutterstock.com; p. 21 LightField Studios/Shutterstock.com.

Names: Pang, Ursula.
Title: Vet / Ursula Pang.
Description: Buffalo, New York : PowerKids Press, 2026. | Series: Health helpers | Includes glossary and index.
Identifiers: ISBN 9781499456585 (pbk.) | ISBN 9781499456592 (library bound) | ISBN 9781499456608 (ebook)
Subjects: LCSH: Veterinarians–Juvenile literature.
Classification: LCC SF756.P36 2026 | DDC 636.089069-dc23

Manufactured in China

CPSIA Compliance Information: Batch #QWPK26. For Further Information contact Rosen Publishing at 1-800-237-9932.

CONTENTS

Animal Doctors

Vets—short for veterinarians—are health helpers for animals! Some vets care for all kinds of small animals. You may take your dog or cat to them if they are sick. Some vets only care for horses or farm animals. Others only care for **reptiles** or birds.

Who's There?

Assistants help vets. They greet people and answer the phone. They clean up after the animals. A worker called a vet tech will likely see your pet before the vet does. Vet techs are vets too, but vets have gone to college for a longer time.

Time for a Check-Up

Pets need a check-up from time to time. The vet tech will weigh your pet. They will ask if the pet has had any problems. The vet will check your pet's ears, mouth, feet, legs, and more. They may give your pet a shot to keep them healthy.

Sick Pets

Dogs and cats can get sick. They can get **fleas** too. Vets know the signs of all kinds of illnesses and know how to treat them. The vet may study your pet's blood. They may need to give your pet a shot or other **medicine** to help them get better.

Animal Injuries

Pets can get injured, or hurt. Vets know how to care for injured animals with care and skill. Vets can treat cuts with **stitches**. They can treat a broken bone with a cast. Vet offices have an **X-ray** machine used to see inside your pet when treating injuries.

X-ray

Animal Surgery

A pet may need to have surgery. This means the vet needs to cut into the animal's body. The pet is given medicine to make it fall asleep. After the surgery, the vet will put a **cone** around the pet's head so they can't bother the surgery area.

Out of the Office

Some vets care for the animals in zoos and aquariums. Wildlife vets help care for wild animals. Large animal vets must go to the animals instead of the animals coming to them! These include farm animals like horses and cows. This way, vets help groups of animals stay healthy.

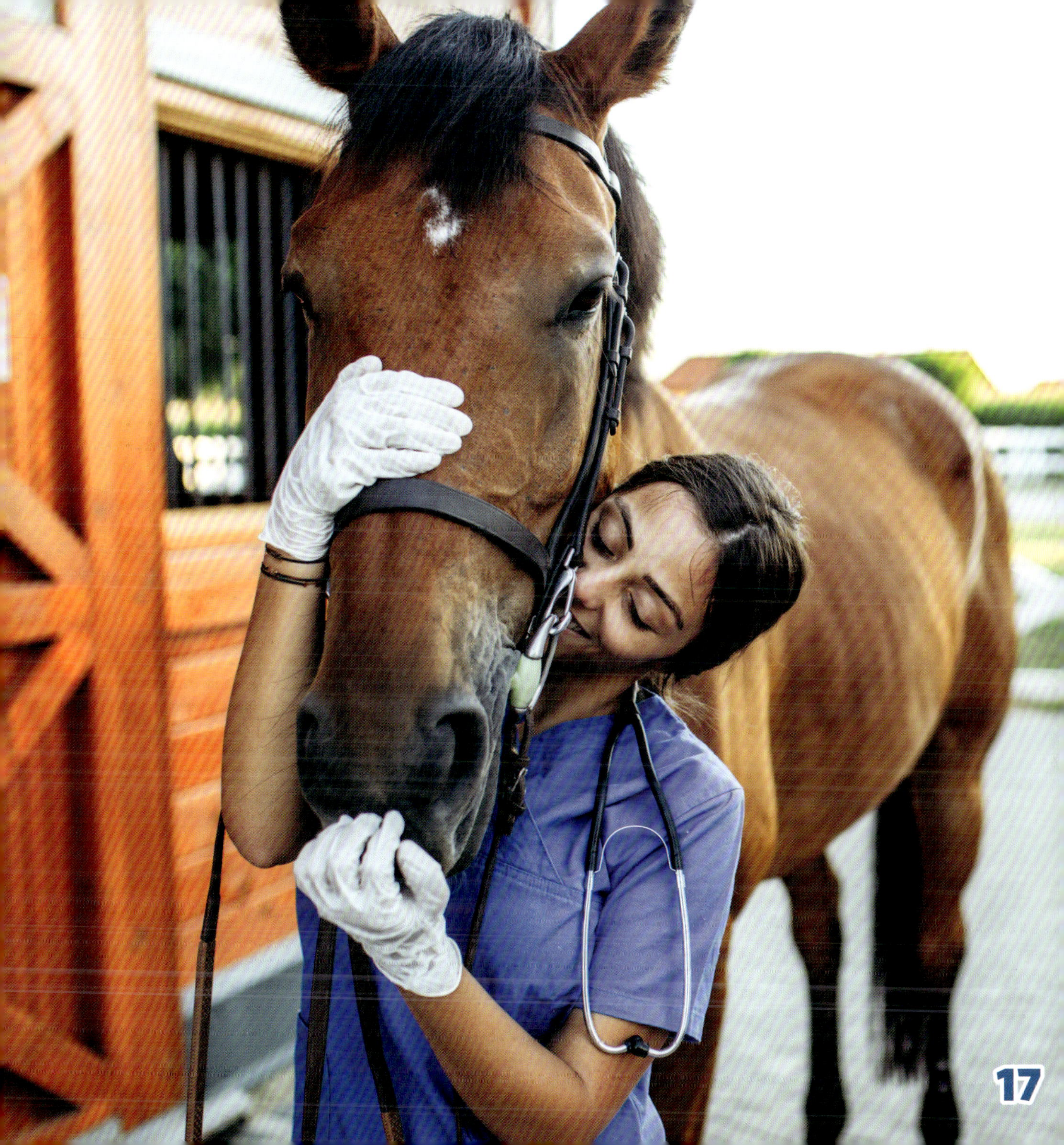

Teaching Others

Vets teach people how to care for their pets. They teach how animals can give illnesses to other animals, and how to stop it from happening. Vets tell people what their pets should eat and what they should not eat. Healthy pets mean fewer trips to the vet!

Healthy Animals!

Vets are animal doctors who make sure our pets are happy and healthy. This keeps pet owners happy and healthy! Vets care about all kinds of animals, from your dogs and cats to animals on a farm or in a zoo. It's hard to think of a world without vets!

GLOSSARY

assistant: A helper.

cone: A plastic guard put on an animal's neck to stop them from biting or licking injuries or stitches.

flea: A tiny bug that feeds on animals' skin.

medicine: A drug that a doctor gives to help fight illness.

reptile: A cold-blooded animal with thin, dry pieces of skin called scales.

stitch: A piece of thread used to close a cut on the skin.

X-ray: Having to do with waves of energy that can go through some parts of the body.

FOR MORE INFORMATION

BOOKS

Honders, Christine. *What's It Really Like to Be a Veterinarian?* Buffalo, NY: PowerKids Press, 2019.

Leed, Percy. *Veterinarians: A First Look*. Minneapolis, MN: Lerner Publishing, 2024.

WEBSITES

Veterinarian Facts for Kids
kids.kiddle.co/Veterinarian
Read a lot more about vets and what they do for you and your pets.

Pet Central
kids.nationalgeographic.com/pages/topic/pet-central
National Geographic Kids has tons of fun information about pets and how to care for them.

INDEX